Project 2025

American Governance

The Battle for Democracy and the Future of

U.S. Politics

Andy S. Rhoden

Copyright

Table of Contents

INTRODUCTION

Project 2025, formally known as the Presidential Transition Project, represents a pivotal initiative spearheaded by the Heritage Foundation, aimed at fundamentally reshaping the landscape of the United States federal government. Founded in 2022 against the backdrop of evolving political dynamics and ideological shifts within the conservative movement, this project stands as a comprehensive blueprint for potential governance should the Republican Party secure victory in the 2024 presidential election.

Beginnings at the Heritage Foundation

Since its founding in 1973, the Heritage Foundation has been a well-known conservative think tank that influences American policy. Promoting classic conservative ideals, limited government, free market, and individual liberty are essential components of its goal. Heritage has released some important studies and policy suggestions throughout the years, such as the "Mandate for Leadership" series, which usually falls around presidential elections. Often referred to as a "policy bible," this series provides comprehensive policy agendas that are in keeping with conservative values for incoming administrations.

The newest edition of Heritage's Mandate for Leadership series, Project 2025, reflects a deliberate attempt to institutionalize what President Kevin Roberts of Heritage has dubbed "Trumpism" in the federal government. Beginning in 2022, the project is a calculated reaction to perceived threats to conservative governance under the Trump administration, especially in light of resistance from firmly established bureaucratic interests and legal challenges to executive orders.

Objectives and Goals

Project 2025's key objectives are to redefine the federal government's function and reach in several different areas. These objectives are supported by a vision to realign government operations with conservative values and to transform the political landscape in a variety of domains, including social policy, national security, healthcare, and taxation.

Restructuring Government Employees and Management:

Reclassifying tens of thousands of federal civil service posts as political appointees is a key component of Project 2025's approach. The purpose of this action is to replace current employees with people who are thought to share conservative values and be devoted to the objectives of the new administration. The project seeks to improve executive authority over federal agencies and expedite decision-making processes by politicizing their responsibilities. This will help to overcome perceived bureaucratic resistance and foster ideological cohesiveness.

Legislative and Policy Agenda:

Project 2025 promotes a thorough legislative agenda to reduce what it considers to be overly intrusive government involvement in the social and economic domains. Proposals to reduce taxes, streamline regulatory frameworks, dissolve or reorganize government agencies, and update healthcare and education programs are all included in this. Proponents of the project contend that these actions are necessary to advance economic development, preserve individual liberties, and uphold what they view as fundamental principles of constitutional governance.

Priorities for National Security and Law Enforcement:

The initiative lays out strong national security measures, with a focus on improved border security, immigration reform, and a review of law enforcement procedures. It presents sweeping reforms to the FBI, the Department of Justice, and military deployment procedures, justifying them as required to counter perceived threats to domestic security and national sovereignty.

Social and Cultural Policy Reforms:

In terms of social policy, Project 2025 promotes a conservative agenda that calls for the abolition of affirmative action initiatives, the restriction of abortion rights, and the reduction of safeguards for LGBTQ+ people. It aims to incorporate Christian nationalism into governmental structures and policies, representing a larger cultural position that upholds moral principles and traditional family values.

Economic and Environmental Policies:

From an economic standpoint, the project supports measures meant to lessen government involvement in the market, cut taxes, and create an environment that encourages the expansion of businesses. It promotes deregulation in areas like energy and environmental protection, contending that doing so will boost employment and economic growth while opposing what it views as onerous environmental laws and climate change initiatives.

Institutional and Cultural Impact:

Project 2025 has important institutional and cultural ramifications for American governance in addition to its policy recommendations. It represents a calculated attempt to institutionalize and solidify a particular ideological agenda within the federal government, which could have a significant impact on judicial rulings, public views of government legitimacy, and bureaucratic standards.

Project 2025 is essentially a daring attempt by conservative forces to seize power inside the federal government and carry out a revolutionary program meant to realign governmental goals with conservative values. As it develops, the project provokes discussion on the nature of the executive branch, the function of government in society, and how to strike a balance between people's rights and their shared responsibilities. While detractors warn of authoritarian tendencies and the deterioration of democratic standards, supporters see it as an essential corrective to what they see as decades of progressive overreach.

CHAPTER 1

FOUNDATIONS OF PROJECT 2025

Historical Context: Heritage Foundation's Mandate for Leadership Series

A mainstay of conservative policy formation in the US is the Heritage Foundation's "Mandate for Leadership" series, which is especially significant during presidential transitions. This series, which began in 1981, not long after Ronald Reagan became president, has functioned as an all-encompassing policy manual to reshape the federal government with conservative values. Every edition of the Mandate for Leadership demonstrates the Foundation's dedication to promoting small government, free business, and traditional American values by outlining detailed policy suggestions in a range of governance sectors, from national security to economic policy.

The show is organized on the idea that the federal government should function within the narrow bounds of the Constitution, with a focus on free markets, individual liberty, and a strong national defense. It has been updated regularly to reflect shifting political environments and conservative regimes' policy agendas. In addition to influencing public opinion, the Mandate for Leadership seeks to direct incoming administrations to enact conservative changes by offering specific policy recommendations. It has become known over the years as a thoroughfare for conservative policy, and during presidential transitions, politicians, academics, and the media frequently cite it.

The Part Kevin Roberts Played in Establishing Trumpism

As president of the Heritage Foundation, Kevin Roberts has been instrumental in establishing the organization's position in contemporary conservative politics, especially in institutionalizing the concept of "Trumpism." Following Donald Trump's surprise ascent to the presidency in 2016, Roberts became leader of Heritage during a period of tremendous political division and doctrinal development within the conservative movement. Strategic efforts to match the Foundation's agenda with the goals and policy preferences expressed by Trump and his allies have been a defining feature of his leadership.

The Heritage Foundation has grown in stature among Republicans under Roberts' direction and established itself as a major source of advice on conservative policy issues. Roberts has highlighted the significance of upholding historic American principles, supporting individual accountability, small government, and a potent national defense. During his leadership, Heritage has actively shaped legislative ideas and shaped public opinion through publications, advocacy campaigns, and research.

Establishing Project 2025 sometimes referred to as the Presidential Transition Project, has been a key component of Roberts' approach. It is a concentrated attempt to get ready for possible conservative rule after the 2024 presidential election. This project offers a comprehensive policy framework designed to direct a future Republican administration in remaking the federal government with conservative ideals, building upon the groundwork established by the Mandate for Leadership series. Roberts and his team hope to guarantee that conservative principles are carried out in a way that is efficient for all government departments and agencies by creating an ideological framework and personnel database.

Roberts' strategy of forming strategic partnerships with influential individuals and groups within the larger conservative movement has been instrumental in institutionalizing Trumpism within the Heritage Foundation. This entails working closely with advisers and officials from the previous Trump administration who are dedicated to furthering conservative policy objectives. Roberts has attempted to close the gap between conservative ideals and the reality of governance, especially in a time of increased political polarization and ideological divide, by utilizing Heritage's intellectual resources and policy skills.

Kevin Roberts's leadership at the Heritage Foundation has been crucial in furthering conservative policy goals and establishing Trumpism as the organization's official position. Roberts, through projects such as the Mandate for Leadership series and Project 2025, has established Heritage as a prominent player in conservative policy discussions and in determining the course of federal governance.

His leadership demonstrates the Foundation's dedication to upholding historic American principles, free business, and limited government while simultaneously adjusting to the changing political environment and conservative movement's policy concerns.

CHAPTER 2

IDEOLOGICAL FRAMEWORK

The Heritage Foundation's Project 2025 is supported by a strong conservative ideological foundation. This chapter examines the conceptual underpinnings of Project 2025 and how it reinterprets constitutional theories in general and the contentious unitary executive idea in particular.

Conservative Thoughts and Values

Fundamentally, Project 2025 represents a conservative worldview that aims to preserve traditional values, restrict the extent of government involvement in the economy and individual rights, and bring back what it considers to be lost moral and cultural standards. This school of thought is mostly influenced by classical conservatism, which emphasizes the value of tradition, hierarchy, and stability in preserving social order.

Limited Government: Supporting limited government is a cornerstone of Project 2025's conservative ideology. Conservatives contend that overzealous government involvement stunts economic expansion and individual liberty. Their primary focus is on diminishing the extent and impact of the federal government, supporting deregulation and the transfer of power to the states.

Fiscal Responsibility: Project 2025's conservative worldview also places a strong emphasis on fiscal discipline. This means promoting balanced budgets, cutting back on government expenditure, and lowering taxes since the idea is that the best way to create economic development is to have as little government intervention in the market as possible.

Traditional Values: Project 2025 gives traditional societal values a lot of weight. These values include encouraging religious freedom, family unity, and a moral code based on Judeo-Christian principles. Conservatives think that these principles are the cornerstone of a morally upright society, and they work to preserve these principles through legislative actions.

National Sovereignty: Project 2025's conservative ideology places a high value on national sovereignty and rejects any foreign alliances or accords that threaten American independence. This includes having doubts about globalist projects and favoring taking trade and national security decisions alone.

Individual Liberty: Project 2025 conservatives support individual liberty and personal responsibility in addition to limited government. They support a laissez-faire style of governance by arguing that people should be allowed to pursue their own economic and social interests without excessive interference from the state.

Constitutional Theory Reinterpreted

The reworking of constitutional theories, notably the unitary executive doctrine, is central to the intellectual framework of Project 2025. According to this viewpoint, the president has broad jurisdiction over the executive branch under the Constitution, including the power to manage administrative agencies and take independent actions without much judicial or legislative review.

Unitary Executive Theory: Project 2025 takes a maximalist stance on the unitary executive theory, claiming that the president has substantial discretionary power over policy decisions in addition to the power to execute legislation. Proponents contend that efficient governance and prompt action—particularly during periods of national emergency or partisan impasse—require this concentration of authority in the executive branch.

Executive Privilege: The idea of executive privilege, which upholds the president's authority to conceal material from Congress or the courts to preserve the privacy of executive branch discussions, is associated with the unitary executive theory. Strong executive privilege safeguards are promoted by Project 2025 as being necessary to maintain the president's independence from unwarranted intervention in his or her decision-making.

Constitutional Interpretation: Project 2025 conservatives support a rigorous constructionist reading of the Constitution, arguing that it should be read by its original meaning and intent when it was drafted. This method differs from judicial activism, which conservatives claim entails judges enforcing their preferred policies while disguising their interpretation of the Constitution.

Separation of Powers: Project 2025 acknowledges the larger framework of separation of powers provided in the Constitution while also arguing for a strong executive. Conservatives contend that to prevent tyranny and guarantee government accountability, it is imperative to preserve separate domains of authority for the legislative, executive, and judicial departments.

Consequences and Reactions

Project 2025's conservative ideological foundation and reworking of constitutional ideas have drawn a lot of discussion and controversy.

Authoritarian Concerns: Project 2025's defenders contend that by adopting a maximalist unitary executive theory, the president may end up with an excessive amount of power, so weakening democratic checks and balances. They bring up issues with authoritarian inclinations and the deterioration of constitutional principles that protect people's liberties and rights.

Rule of Law: Project 2025's reworking of constitutional doctrines has drawn criticism from some legal professors and political observers who believe it could weaken the rule of law. They contend that sweeping conceptions of executive power may give rise to constitutional crises, institutional disputes, and legal disputes, especially if actions taken by the president are thought to go beyond constitutional bounds.

Political Polarization: Project 2025's conservative tenets fuel political divisiveness by endorsing policies that stand in stark contrast to liberal or progressive ideas about politics, society, and international affairs. This ideological gap feeds divisive discussions in the courts, Congress, and public discourse.

Project 2025's Chapter 2 explores the ideologies that inform its proposed policies and constitutional interpretations. Project 2025 aims to restructure federal governance through a rigorous reworking of the unitary executive idea, embracing conservative principles of limited government, fiscal responsibility, traditional values, and national sovereignty. While supporters stress the need for strong leadership and efficient government, detractors point out issues with authoritarianism, the integrity of the constitution, and the possible deterioration of democratic standards. The enormous consequences of Project 2025's vision for the political environment and constitutional governance of America are highlighted by this ideological conflict.

CHAPTER 3

GOVERNMENT PERSONNEL AND CONTROL

Reclassifying federal civil servant positions as political appointees is a proposed change.

One of the more divisive ideas in Project 2025 is to reclassify tens of thousands of federal civil servant positions as political appointees. With this plan, professional civil servants will be replaced with conservatives who will be more devoted to the goals and policies of the incoming administration. This proposal's justification is part of a deliberate attempt to alter the federal government's personnel so that it more closely embodies and advances conservative values throughout its many departments and agencies.

An Overview of Political and Civil Service Appointments

For stability, competence, and continuity in governance, the U.S. government must distinguish between political appointees and civil servants. Traditionally, civil workers are hired based on their skills, experience, and competence rather than their political affiliation. This is accomplished through a merit-based system. Regardless of shifts in the political leadership, they are supposed to maintain the rule of law and serve with impartiality.

On the other hand, political appointees are chosen, usually at the start of a new administration, by elected politicians or their designees. The president appoints these individuals, and they are in charge of carrying out the goals and policies of the administration. Even while they provide political alignment and guidance for policy, political appointees frequently lack the in-depth institutional knowledge and expertise of career civil servants.

Justification for Reclassification

Project 2025 is in favor of reclassifying civil service jobs to better ensure that the administration's program is carried out more cogently and to bring the federal workforce into line with conservative values. Among the justifications are:

Alignment of Ideology: The strategy seeks to guarantee that those in important positions share the conservative ideals of the administration by transforming civil service jobs into political appointments. It is believed that this alignment is essential to overcoming any potential institutional resistance among the career civil service levels to conservative policies.

Enhanced Accountability: Proponents contend that political appointees have a greater responsibility to the administration and its policies, which expedites the execution of policies and lessens bureaucratic inertia. It is believed that this accountability is essential to passing major policy changes quickly, especially in sectors where entrenched bureaucracy is expected to resist.

Strategic Maneuverability: The administration has more leeway in reclassifying civil service positions to better tailor the federal government's workforce to achieve its particular policy goals. It makes it possible to assign people who actively promote conservative policy proposals in addition to those who just support them, which could have an impact on agency decision-making processes.

Implications for Government Agencies

The idea of reclassifying positions held by civil servants as political appointees has important ramifications for the integrity and operation of government agencies:

Deterioration of Expertise and Non-Partisanship

Historically, civil service positions have been shielded from political influence to preserve their impartiality and proficiency in managing government services and projects. Declaring these posts to be filled by political appointees runs the risk of politicizing organizations that are normally in charge of enforcing laws and regulations in an unbiased manner. This change may make it harder for the public to trust government agencies to act in the public interest rather than just political interests, undermining the agencies' perceived neutrality.

Impact on Knowledge Within Institutions

Professional public servants frequently have extensive institutional knowledge and experience that they have built up through years of work. If these positions are changed to political appointees, agency continuity and efficiency may be disrupted by employee turnover and the loss of experienced staff. Effective governance and decision-making may be hampered by institutional memory loss, especially during administration changes.

Possibility of Cronyism and Patronage

Concerns of cronyism and patronage within government agencies are raised by political appointments made based on allegiance rather than merit. Opponents contend that such actions could undermine the merit-based recruitment criteria for public service by giving political ties precedence over competence. Career public servant morale may suffer as a result, and they may become less motivated to carry out their tasks impartially.

Challenges to Civil Service Benefits

The purpose of civil service safeguards is to shield federal workers from politically motivated dismissals or unjust terminations. These safeguards might be weakened if civil service posts were reclassified as political appointees, putting workers at risk of increased employment instability due to shifting political winds. This might discourage gifted people from entering the public sector and reduce the efficacy of the federal workforce as a whole.

Pressure on the Efficiency of Government

A large number of civil service positions must be converted to political appointees, which means hiring, screening, and integrating new hires will take time and money. This procedure could interfere with agency operations and take focus away from important government duties, especially when it comes to enacting policies and handling crises. The perceived advantages in efficiency and policy alignment may be outweighed by the logistical difficulties of such a shift.

The Project 2025 proposal to reclassify federal civil servant positions as political appointees signifies a significant change in the federal government of the United States' governance framework. Supporters contend that it is imperative to bring conservative values to the federal workforce and improve the way policies are implemented, but detractors warn about the government agencies' institutional integrity, expertise, and neutrality being compromised. Such a policy shift has ramifications that go beyond issues of administrative effectiveness and include more general issues of democratic governance, accountability, and the place of experts in public service. The future of American governance continues to depend on striking a balance between political accountability and institutional stability, a topic of discussion around the future course of federal personnel policy.

CHAPTER 4

LEGISLATIVE AGENDA

In Project 2025, the legislative agenda outlines a sweeping array of policy proposals aimed at fundamentally reshaping the economic and social landscape of the United States. This chapter delves into two critical areas of focus: tax policy reforms and healthcare and education policy changes. These areas not only reflect the ideological underpinnings of the conservative vision but also highlight the contentious debates surrounding fiscal responsibility, government intervention, and social welfare.

Tax Policy Reforms: Cuts, Simplifications, and Protectionism Debates

Tax Cuts and Simplifications

A comprehensive agenda of tax reforms aimed at encouraging investment, boosting economic growth, and lowering the overall tax burden on individuals and corporations is the cornerstone of Project 2025's economic policy. To improve compliance and efficiency, the project promotes simplification of the tax system in addition to large reductions across some tax areas.

Individual income tax rates will be reduced to two bands under the proposed reforms: a 15% rate for most income levels and a 30% rate for incomes over a certain threshold, most likely linked to the Social Security Wage Base. The goal of this dual-tier structure is to establish a flatter tax system, which supporters claim will encourage entrepreneurship and consumer spending by giving taxpayers more discretionary money.

Reductions in corporate tax rates are also a goal; Project 2025 suggests bringing the statutory rate down to 18%. Proponents contend that this change is essential for boosting American competitiveness abroad, drawing in investment, and motivating companies to repatriate profits they currently hold abroad. The justification for these reductions is consistent with conventional conservative economic theory, which holds that reduced tax rates encourage corporate investment, job growth, and economic progress.

Protectionism Debates

Project 2025's economic framework is controversial because of its position on protectionism. While some project supporters support greater tariffs as a way to level the playing field in global commerce, others warn about the possible unfavorable effects of protectionist measures. The arguments about protectionism are a reflection of larger divisions within the conservative movement over the best way to strike a balance between defending homegrown companies and free trade principles.

Tariffs on imported goods, according to proponents of protectionism, are required to shield American companies and workers from unfair competition, especially from countries with laxer regulations and labor standards. They contend that taking these steps is necessary to close trade gaps, support homegrown industry, and improve national security by lowering reliance on foreign supply chains.

Protectionist policies, according to their detractors, could have unintended consequences such as inciting trade partner retaliation, upsetting global supply networks, and driving up consumer costs for imported goods. They contend that by lowering costs and facilitating access to a greater variety of goods and services, free trade ultimately benefits American firms and consumers by fostering economic efficiency, innovation, and consumer choice.

Project 2025's protectionism discussions highlight the intricacies of trade policy and the difficulty of striking a balance between free market economics and economic nationalism. In the event that a Republican administration takes office after 2024, these discussions will probably have an impact on the project's legislative priorities and strategy for handling international trade relations.

Healthcare and Education Policy Changes

Affordable Care Act (ACA) and Healthcare Reform

Project 2025 suggests substantial alterations to the healthcare system, specifically focusing on the Affordable Care Act (ACA), also referred to as Obamacare. Concerns about government overreach, rising healthcare prices, and restrictions on consumer choice are used by the project to support its repeal and replacement of the Affordable Care Act.

Destroying the employer and individual mandates of the Affordable Care Act (ACA), which impose fines on companies and individuals for failing to obtain health insurance, is one of Project 2025's main goals.

Advocates contend that these regulations restrict personal freedoms and place excessive financial strain on companies, hindering economic expansion and creativity.

Project 2025 advocates for a market-driven approach to healthcare reform in lieu of the Affordable Care Act (ACA), placing special emphasis on increased access to health savings accounts (HSAs) as alternatives to standard health insurance plans, pricing transparency, and competition among insurance providers. Proponents contend that giving patients more options and flexibility will save costs, enhance care quality, and encourage innovation in medical devices and therapies.

However, opponents caution that millions of Americans may become uninsured or underinsured if the Affordable Care Act is repealed without a comprehensive replacement plan. This is especially true for people with pre-existing diseases who depend on the ACA's protections for coverage. They contend that the ACA has improved health outcomes, especially for low-income and vulnerable groups, decreased coverage inequities, and increased access to healthcare for millions of Americans.

Department of Education (DOE) and Education Reform

The Department of Education (DOE) and its influence over federal education policy are a central focus of Project 2025's legislative agenda. The project makes the case that the DOE should be abolished or drastically restructured because it is too big, too bureaucratic, and too inefficient to meet the requirements of teachers and students.

Proponents of DOE reform within Project 2025 suggest giving state and local governments control over education policy and financing duties in order to decentralize decision-making and boost community responsibility. They contend that local control encourages competition among schools to improve academic achievements, encourages innovation, and allows educators to customize curricula to fit the requirements of a varied student body.

Project 2025 promotes K–12 education changes in addition to reorganizing the DOE. These reforms include extending school choice programs like vouchers, charter schools, and education savings accounts (ESAs). Proponents contend that these programs address educational opportunity gaps, encourage academic performance, and give parents more influence over their kids' education.

Decentralizing education policy, according to critics of DOE reform, may amplify already-existing disparities in financing and resources between wealthy and underprivileged communities, hence increasing achievement gaps and sustaining structural imbalances in the educational system. They contend that maintaining civil rights protections in schools, assisting disadvantaged student populations, and guaranteeing equitable access to high-quality education all depend on government financing and oversight.

Chapter 4 of Project 2025 presents a comprehensive legislative agenda that aims to fundamentally alter the American economy, social policy, and governance. The agenda demonstrates the ideological division and policy priorities within the conservative movement. It ranges from tax policy reforms targeted at encouraging fiscal conservatism and economic growth to healthcare and education policy changes focused on limiting government intervention and empowering individual choice.

The suggested changes, meanwhile, are not without controversy. Opponents contend that they could worsen social inequality, jeopardize public health and education programs, and erode regulatory safeguards. As a result, they are expected to encounter strong resistance. The discussions surrounding healthcare reform, tax reduction, protectionism, and changes to education policies bring to light the difficult decisions and trade-offs involved in implementing comprehensive legislative reforms that attempt to radically transform the role of government in society.

The results of these discussions, which represent divergent perspectives on the country's economic prosperity, healthcare system, and educational opportunities, will determine the course of American governance and social welfare policies going forward as Project 2025 continues to develop and possibly influence policy discussions preceding the 2024 presidential election.

CHAPTER 5

LAW ENFORCEMENT AND NATIONAL SECURITY

Under Project 2025's ambitious design, rebuilding the federal government around power over law enforcement and national security agencies is a key component. This chapter explores the proposed changes to immigration laws, border security programs, military deployment for domestic law enforcement, the Department of Justice (DOJ), and the Federal Bureau of Investigation (FBI). The recommendations put out are indicative of a strategic realignment with conservative values and ambitions, reiterating the larger themes of allegiance and ideological homogeneity that Project 2025 has in mind.

Department of Justice (DOJ) and Federal Bureau of Investigation (FBI)

Central to Project 2025's vision is the reformation of the DOJ and FBI, institutions historically charged with upholding the rule of law and ensuring justice impartiality. The project advocates for partisan control over these agencies, emphasizing the appointment of officials who align closely with conservative values and the agenda of the sitting Republican president. This proposal marks a departure from traditional norms of governance, where independence and professionalism within law enforcement are prioritized.

Under Project 2025, the leadership of the DOJ and FBI would be reshaped to reflect a stricter adherence to conservative principles in law enforcement and judicial proceedings. This includes the appointment of attorneys general and directors of the FBI who are explicitly committed to policies such as stringent enforcement of immigration laws, crackdowns on perceived threats to national security, and alignment with conservative social values on issues like abortion and LGBTQ+ rights.

Critics argue that such partisan control could undermine the impartiality of these agencies, potentially politicizing law enforcement decisions and judicial proceedings. The project's proponents, however, assert that aligning these agencies with conservative values is essential to rectify what they perceive as years of progressive overreach in law enforcement under previous administrations.

Military Deployment for Domestic Law Enforcement

Project 2025's support for increased military participation in domestic law enforcement operations is one of its controversial aspects. The initiative suggests using the Insurrection Act of 1807, a seldom used statute that gives the president the authority to send federal troops inside the borders of the United States to put down revolt, insurrection, or civil unrest. The proper role of the military in domestic law enforcement as well as how to strike a balance between civil liberties and national security have become hot topics of discussion in response to this suggestion.

Proponents contend that in situations of extensive public disturbance or dangers deemed existential to national security, such actions are necessary to restore order. They cite other instances in history, like the civil rights movement or more recent demonstrations against racial injustice and police brutality, where military intervention was used. Advocates for Project 2025 contend that upholding law and order is essential to safeguarding American neighborhoods and maintaining the country's unity.

Critics, however, warn against the militarization of law enforcement because to possible abuses of authority, violations of civil rights, and deterioration of democratic standards. They contend that the use of military force domestically runs the risk of escalating hostilities and eroding public confidence in political institutions, especially when it comes to the use of force against marginalized groups or nonviolent protestors.

Immigration Policy Reforms

Immigration policy reform stands as a cornerstone of Project 2025's agenda, reflecting a hardline stance on border security and undocumented immigration. The project proposes sweeping changes aimed at curbing illegal immigration, tightening border security measures, and overhauling the legal immigration system to prioritize skills-based criteria and national interest considerations.

Key proposals include:

Border Security Enhancements: Project 2025 advocates for significant investments in physical barriers along the U.S.-Mexico border, enhanced surveillance technologies, and increased funding for

Border Patrol operations. This includes bolstering Border Patrol personnel and resources to deter illegal crossings and smuggling activities.

Interior Enforcement: The project calls for stringent enforcement measures within the United States, including ramped-up workplace inspections, penalties for employers hiring undocumented workers, and increased collaboration between federal agencies and local law enforcement to identify and deport undocumented individuals.

Asylum and Refugee Policies: Under Project 2025, asylum and refugee policies would undergo substantial revisions, with stricter eligibility criteria and expedited processing procedures aimed at reducing backlogs and deterring fraudulent claims. The project also advocates for regional partnerships and agreements to address the root causes of migration and enhance border security cooperation.

These reforms are framed within the broader narrative of national security and economic protectionism, asserting that controlling immigration flows is essential to safeguarding American jobs, reducing crime rates, and preserving cultural cohesion. Proponents argue that stricter enforcement measures are necessary to uphold the rule of law and ensure fair treatment for legal immigrants and citizens.

Critics counter that Project 2025's immigration proposals risk exacerbating humanitarian crises, separating families, and perpetuating systemic injustices against vulnerable populations. They argue for comprehensive immigration reform that balances enforcement with compassion, addresses the root causes of migration, and upholds international humanitarian obligations.

Border Security Proposals

Aligned with its immigration policy reforms, Project 2025 outlines comprehensive border security proposals aimed at fortifying U.S. borders against illegal immigration, drug trafficking, and other transnational threats. These proposals include:

Physical Barriers: Advocacy for the construction of a border wall along the U.S.-Mexico border, citing it as a critical deterrent to unauthorized crossings and criminal activities. Project 2025 proposes substantial investments in border infrastructure to enhance security and control access points.

Technological Advancements: Emphasis on deploying state-of-the-art surveillance technologies, drones, and sensors to monitor border regions effectively. The project calls for partnerships with private sector innovators to develop and implement cutting-edge solutions for border security challenges.

Personnel and Resources: Expansion of Border Patrol personnel, training programs, and operational resources to improve response times, intelligence gathering capabilities, and interagency coordination. Project 2025 advocates for increased funding allocations to support border security initiatives and enhance law enforcement presence in border regions.

These border security proposals are presented as essential measures to safeguard national sovereignty, protect American communities from external threats, and uphold the integrity of immigration laws. Proponents argue that securing U.S. borders is a fundamental responsibility of the federal government, crucial for maintaining public safety and defending against illicit activities.

Critics raise concerns about the effectiveness and cost-effectiveness of such measures, questioning the feasibility of a border wall and highlighting potential environmental and humanitarian impacts. They advocate for alternative approaches to border security that prioritize humanitarian values, diplomatic engagement, and collaborative solutions with neighboring countries.

Chapter 5 of Project 2025's mandate for leadership reflects a comprehensive strategy to overhaul law enforcement and national security policies in alignment with conservative principles. From restructuring the DOJ and FBI to advocating for expanded military involvement in domestic law enforcement, immigration policy reforms, and stringent border security measures, the proposals outlined in this chapter underscore a fundamental shift in governance priorities. While proponents argue for restoring law and order, enhancing national security, and controlling immigration flows, critics warn of potential risks to civil liberties, democratic norms, and international relations. The implementation of these policies would undoubtedly shape the future trajectory of American governance, prompting ongoing debates over the balance between security imperatives and individual rights in a democratic society.

CHAPTER 6

SOCIAL AND CULTURAL POLICIES

Social and cultural policies proposed under Project 2025 reflect a conservative agenda aimed at reshaping societal norms and values according to traditionalist principles. This chapter delves into the project's positions on key issues such as abortion, LGBTQ+ rights, diversity programs, and the contentious proposal to criminalize pornography, examining their potential impacts on civil liberties and broader societal dynamics.

Abortion Guidelines

Project 2025 advocates for a dramatic rollback of the reproductive rights established after Roe v. Wade, which is central to the organization's social agenda. The project seeks to limit access to reproductive services across the United States and vehemently condemns abortion as medical care. The proposal advocates for the preservation of fetal rights from conception onward and suggests legal measures that would essentially outlaw the majority of abortions.

The goal of the policy framework is to stop funding Planned Parenthood and other organizations that perform abortions and instead, direct funds to crisis pregnancy centers that support non-abortion options. Furthermore, Project 2025 proposes to nominate judges who share its anti-abortion views, which could result in legal challenges meant to overturn or severely restrict Roe v. Wade.

Opponents contend that implementing such policies would violate women's right to reproductive autonomy and unfairly harm underprivileged populations with little access to medical treatment. Concerns are expressed regarding the proposal's potential to undermine long-standing rights and bring dangerous, covert abortion procedures back to jurisdictions where access to abortion is severely restricted.

LGBTQ+ Rights and Policies

Project 2025 takes a conservative stance toward LGBTQ+ rights, prioritizing religious freedom and traditional family values over increased civil rights for the LGBTQ+ community. The initiative argues that laws against discrimination based on gender identity and sexual orientation violate religious freedom and threaten traditional family units. As a result, it is against these laws.

Reversing recent advances in LGBTQ+ rights, such as the Equality Act, which aims to give LGBTQ+ people federal civil rights protections, is part of the policy agenda. Rather, Project 2025 supports state-level authority over LGBTQ+ rights matters, enabling local governments to establish laws that align with their conservative principles.

LGBTQ+ advocacy organizations and allies have strongly criticized this position, claiming that it upholds discrimination and inequality. Critics argue that the Constitution's tenets of inclusiveness and equality are compromised when people are denied equal protection under the law because of their gender identity or sexual orientation.

Affirmative Action and Diversity Initiatives

Project 2025 criticizes affirmative action and diversity programs that attempt to correct historical injustices and advance diversity in the workplace and educational institutions, in keeping with its larger conservative ideology. The initiative makes the case that by giving preference to race, gender, and other demographic characteristics over qualifications, such programs reinforce identity politics and undercut the ideas of merit-based education.

Project 2025's recommendations call for cutting federal support for affirmative action and diversity training programs in favor of programs that put meritocracy and individual success first. Proponents of these policies contend that they are necessary to remove systemic barriers that marginalized communities experience and to create inclusive environments.

Opponents argue that eliminating diversity initiatives could worsen inequality and impede the advancement of fairness and representation. They contend that diversity initiatives—especially in fields where historical underrepresentation still exists—are essential to advancing an equitable and inclusive society.

Criminalization of Pornography

The idea that pornography should be made illegal by Project 2025, which frames it as a moral and public health concern, is one of the social agenda's more contentious elements. The project raises worries about pornography's alleged negative consequences on people and society and pushes for strict legislation that would forbid its creation, dissemination, and consumption.

Proponents of the plan contend that moral decline, the objectification of women, and unfavorable public perceptions of sexuality are all caused by pornography. They argue that to preserve traditional values and safeguard public morality—especially with regard to family and community standards—pornography must be made illegal.

Critics of such policies, however, raise serious concerns about civil freedoms. They contend that making pornography illegal violates the First Amendment's guarantees of free speech and privacy. Furthermore, they draw attention to the possibility that laws that outlaw the sector could push it underground, resulting in the emergence of more exploitative and uncontrolled pornography.

The argument over whether or not pornography should be illegal touches on more general topics such as censorship, personal freedom, and the role of government in controlling conduct. Adults should be free to consume any lawful information they want without interference from the government, according to opponents, as long as it doesn't hurt other people or break any laws already in place.

Implications for Civil Rights

The social and cultural reforms that Project 2025 is proposing raise serious questions about how they may affect American civil liberties. The project's agenda questions accepted conventions and legal safeguards that preserve individual liberty, including freedom of expression, LGBTQ+ equality, and reproductive rights.

Critics caution that the weakening of LGBTQ+ and reproductive rights provisions may create a hazardous precedent for reversing civil rights victories won over many years of campaigning and court cases. They contend that restricting these rights in the name of moral conservatism or religious freedom endangers vulnerable groups and threatens the foundations of legal equality.

Proposals to curtail affirmative action and diversity programs may also impede chances for historically excluded groups and sustain systemic imbalances. Promoting diversity and inclusion, according to civil rights advocates, is crucial to creating a just and equitable society that recognizes the contributions of every person, regardless of color, gender, or sexual orientation.

Discussions about pornography revolve around striking a balance between moral principles and constitutional guarantees of free speech. Legislative regulation of private sexual behavior, according to opponents of criminalization, not only infringes on people's right to privacy but also ignores deeper social problems with consent and sexuality.

The social and cultural initiatives of Project 2025 are the result of a determined attempt to mold American society by moral ideals and conservative beliefs. Redefining public morality and personal liberty, the project's aim ranges from opposing LGBTQ+ rights and diversity initiatives to restricting abortion.

The idea to make pornography illegal highlights larger discussions over the role of the state in controlling individual conduct and defending civil liberties. The possible effects of these regulations on societal norms and individual liberties are still hotly contested issues as they develop and come under examination.

The United States must make important choices regarding how to strike a balance between moral conservatism and constitutional guarantees of individual rights as it navigates these complicated challenges. For many years to come, the results of these discussions will influence social policy and civil freedoms in the nation.

This chapter examines how Project 2025's suggested social and cultural policies can drastically change American law and society and spark heated discussions about core principles.

CHAPTER 7

ECONOMIC POLICIES

In the ambitious blueprint of Project 2025, economic policies stand as pillars intended to reshape the United States' economic landscape drastically. This chapter delves into the proposed corporate tax cuts, regulation rollbacks, and trade policy reforms, alongside the contentious energy policies focusing on fossil fuels, climate change skepticism, and environmental regulations. These initiatives not only outline a conservative economic vision but also ignite debates over their potential impacts on economic growth, environmental sustainability, and global relations.

Corporate Tax Cuts and Regulatory Rollbacks

Corporate Tax Policy:

The centerpiece of Project 2025's economic plan is a significant reform of corporation taxes, modeled after previous Republican initiatives but with greater fervor. By drastically decreasing rates and cutting the number of tax brackets, the idea aims to simplify the tax code. Project 2025 specifically suggests lowering the corporate tax rate to 18%, seeing the current rate as harmful to competitiveness and economic growth. As per the conventional conservative economic theory, which links tax reduction to higher corporate investment and economic dynamism, the reduction in taxes is intended to encourage investment, create jobs, and enhance overall economic productivity.

These tax cuts have more justification than simple economic stimulation. Proponents contend that companies will have more money to innovate, grow domestically, and maintain their competitiveness in the global market if the corporate tax burden is reduced. Additionally, supporters contend that lowering corporate rates will draw in foreign capital, strengthening American leadership in the world economy.

Regulatory Rollbacks:

Project 2025 promotes considerable regulatory rollbacks in some economic areas in addition to tax reduction. The program aims to reduce what it considers to be onerous rules from the government that hinder the expansion and creativity of businesses. This movement toward deregulatory measures includes, among other things, labor legislation, financial sector supervision, and environmental rules. Reducing regulatory barriers, according to supporters, will provide companies with more flexibility, cheaper compliance costs, and more profitability, all of which will contribute to more strong economic growth and job creation.

Opponents, however, warn about the possible negative effects of deregulatory policies, citing hazards including worker exploitation, environmental damage, and unstable finances. They contend that overturning laws intended to safeguard the environment, public health, and safety could have long-term negative effects on society and erode public confidence in governmental institutions.

Trade Policy and Protectionism

Trade Policy Reforms:

To reduce trade imbalances and safeguard American companies, Project 2025 emphasizes protectionist measures as part of its call for a rethink of U.S. trade policy. This strategy highlights a renewed emphasis on economic nationalism and stands in stark contrast to the cosmopolitan inclinations of prior administrations. One of the main recommendations is to increase import duties on goods coming from nations thought to be involved in unfair trade practices, especially China.

Protectionism's proponents contend that it will save American employment, boost homegrown businesses, and lessen reliance on imports. They argue that earlier free trade deals hurt American workers and caused manufacturing jobs to be offshored, which exacerbated economic inequality and stagnation in some areas of the nation.

Debates on Protectionism:

However, critics warn that protectionist measures could trigger retaliatory tariffs from trading partners, escalate trade tensions globally, and disrupt international supply chains. Moreover, they argue that protectionism may lead to higher consumer prices, reduced consumer choice, and overall economic inefficiency. Critics also point to historical precedents where protectionist policies have failed to deliver long-term economic benefits and have instead exacerbated economic downturns.

Energy Policy: Focus on Fossil Fuels and Climate Change Skepticism

Fossil Fuel Emphasis:

A cornerstone of Project 2025's energy policy is its strong emphasis on expanding domestic production of fossil fuels, including oil, natural gas, and coal. The initiative proposes to roll back regulations perceived as hindrances to fossil fuel extraction and development, such as those imposed by the Environmental Protection Agency (EPA) and other federal agencies. Proponents argue that increasing domestic energy production will enhance energy independence, create jobs in the energy sector, and reduce reliance on foreign oil imports.

Climate Change Skepticism:

Project 2025 reflects skepticism towards mainstream climate science and proposes policies that question the severity and human causation of climate change. This skepticism is evident in the initiative's recommendations to repeal or weaken environmental regulations aimed at mitigating greenhouse gas emissions and combating climate change. For instance, the project suggests withdrawing from international agreements like the Paris Climate Accord and scaling back funding for climate research and renewable energy initiatives.

Critics view this stance as detrimental to global efforts to combat climate change, citing scientific consensus on the human impact on the climate and the urgent need for coordinated action to reduce greenhouse gas emissions. They argue that failing to address climate change could lead to catastrophic environmental consequences, including rising sea levels, extreme weather events, and threats to global food security.

Environmental Regulations and Consequences

Rollback of Environmental Regulations:

Project 2025 suggests considerable regulatory reductions in several industries related to the environment, in addition to encouraging the production of fossil fuels. These include lowering automobile emissions regulations, easing industrial pollution controls, and reducing the power of environmental agencies to impose rigorous environmental regulations. Proponents claim that by reducing compliance costs and restrictions on firms, these regulatory measures will boost economic growth in energy-intensive industries.

Environmental and Social Implications:

Critics worry that if environmental laws are weakened, there may be more pollution in the air and water, damage to habitats, and threats to the public's health. They contend that environmental regulations are necessary to preserve biodiversity, natural resources, and community health across the United States. Critics further argue that if the United States does not take action on climate change, it could damage its reputation internationally and increase tensions over environmental stewardship.

The economic ideas of Project 2025 offer a daring vision for restructuring the American economy through regulatory rollbacks, corporate tax cuts, and a concentration on fossil fuels in the face of pessimism about climate change. Critics caution against possible environmental degradation, economic volatility, and international ramifications, while supporters defend these actions as essential for national sovereignty and economic renewal. The chapter highlights the significant ideological and practical ramifications of Project 2025's economic agenda, laying the groundwork for divisive discussions over the future course of US economic policy and its position as a global leader in the twenty-first century.

CHAPTER 8

RELIGIOUS INFLUENCE IN GOVERNANCE

Promotion of Christian Nationalism and Its Role in Policy Decisions

Project 2025, spearheaded by the Heritage Foundation, presents a bold vision for reshaping American governance under a conservative agenda. Central to this vision is the promotion of Christian nationalism, a concept that intertwines religious values with political governance. Christian nationalism, as articulated within Project 2025, posits that America is fundamentally a Christian nation and seeks to elevate Christian principles and beliefs into various facets of public policy.

Historical Context and Development

The roots of Christian nationalism in American politics can be traced back to the country's founding, where religious values often influenced the formation of laws and governance structures. However, its resurgence in modern politics, particularly within conservative circles, has been notable. Project 2025 represents a concentrated effort to institutionalize Christian values within governmental policies, drawing from a narrative that sees Christianity as integral to American identity and governance.

Policy Implications

Within the framework of Project 2025, Christian nationalism manifests in several policy proposals across social, cultural, and educational domains. These include:

Social Policies: Advocacy for legislation that aligns with conservative Christian views on issues such as abortion, LGBTQ+ rights, and family values. Project 2025 aims to overturn progressive policies and legal protections deemed contrary to Christian teachings, positioning these changes as essential for moral governance.

Education: Proposal to reform the educational system to promote Christian principles in curriculum and school practices. This includes potential measures to limit or eliminate teaching materials perceived as contradicting Christian values, such as certain aspects of sex education or discussions on gender identity.

Cultural Influence: Support for initiatives that reinforce Christian symbolism and traditions in public life, challenging the separation of church and state principles. This may involve endorsing religious displays in government buildings or ceremonies that invoke Christian rituals or prayers.

Legal Framework: Advocacy for legal interpretations and decisions that favor religious freedoms over perceived encroachments by secularism. Project 2025 seeks to appoint judges and legal officials sympathetic to Christian nationalist perspectives, aiming to reshape the judiciary's stance on issues related to religious expression and state neutrality.

Public Reception and Controversies

The promotion of Christian nationalism within Project 2025 has sparked significant controversy and debate. Critics argue that privileging Christianity in governance violates the principle of separation of church and state enshrined in the First Amendment of the U.S. Constitution. They contend that such policies could marginalize religious minorities and infringe upon individuals' rights to freedom of belief and expression.

Support and Opposition

Project 2025 proponents of Christian nationalism see it as an essential counterbalance to what they see as a secular drift in American culture. They contend that in addition to being constitutionally legitimate, recognizing America's Christian origins and beliefs is crucial for upholding social norms and morals. Additionally, proponents claim that allowing Christians' views to influence public policy protects religious people's freedom to engage fully in society without surrendering their moral principles.

On the other hand, detractors, such as civil rights organizations and proponents of religious liberty, express apprehensions regarding the exclusive character of giving preference to a certain theological perspective over others. They issue a warning about possible prejudice and the demise of pluralism in a society that is multicultural. They also emphasize the significance of upholding a secular government that fairly respects a range of religious and nonreligious viewpoints.

Separation of Church and State Debates Within Project 2025

Constitutional Foundations and Interpretations

The concept of separation of church and state, although not explicitly mentioned in the U.S. Constitution, has been interpreted by courts and legal scholars as a fundamental principle to prevent government endorsement or interference in religious matters. Project 2025's approach to this principle reflects a contentious interpretation that seeks to redefine the boundaries between religion and governance.

Legal Challenges and Proposals

Project 2025 proposes several measures that challenge traditional interpretations of the separation of church and state:

Legislative Initiatives: Advocacy for laws that accommodate religious practices and beliefs in public spaces and institutions, potentially allowing for exemptions or special considerations based on religious convictions.

Judicial Appointments: Emphasis on appointing judges and legal advisors who share a sympathetic view towards accommodating religious expressions in governmental activities. This includes revisiting landmark cases that have shaped the legal framework around religious freedoms and state neutrality.

Executive Actions: Potential executive orders or administrative directives that promote religious symbols or observances in governmental settings, presenting a proactive stance on integrating religious values into public policy.

Impact on Governance and Society

The implementation of Project 2025's proposals regarding the separation of church and state could have far-reaching implications for governance and societal cohesion:

Legal Precedents: Changes in legal precedents and interpretations could redefine the balance between religious freedoms and state obligations, influencing future court decisions and legislative debates.

Social Cohesion: Potential divisions within society based on religious affiliations and beliefs, as policies favoring Christian nationalism may alienate religious minorities and secular individuals.

Constitutional Integrity: Debates over the constitutionality of Project 2025's initiatives could shape public discourse on the role of religion in public life and the limits of governmental authority.

A notable divergence from conventional understandings of the separation of church and state in American politics is the advocacy of Christian nationalism within Project 2025. It promotes laws that subvert accepted social norms and legal structures in favor of elevating Christian ideals and beliefs into official government procedures. The discussions around these plans bring up important issues about pluralism, religious freedom, and the constitutional limits on state power. Project 2025's effects on American politics and societal norms will continue to be closely watched and hotly debated as it develops.

This chapter explores the intricate relationship between religion and governance in Project 2025, looking at its ramifications, debates, and wider social effects.

CHAPTER 9

CRITICISMS AND LEGAL CHALLENGES

With its bold plan to restructure the federal government according to conservative ideals, Project 2025 has not been without criticism and controversy. This chapter explores the major objections raised against the project, with an emphasis on worries about the project's potential for authoritarian inclinations, the deterioration of democratic norms, and potential legal issues brought on by its suggested policies.

Deterioration of Democratic Norms and Authoritarian Tendencies

Many of Project 2025's recommendations, according to its detractors, are more in line with authoritarian tendencies than with democratic governance ideals.

The project's support of a maximalist reading of the unitary executive theory, which maintains broad presidential powers over the executive branch, lies at the heart of these concerns. Although it is controversial, this theory seeks to consolidate power in the hands of the president upon inauguration by undermining the conventional checks and balances found in the U.S. Constitution.

Expansion of Presidential Powers: The project's critics claim it is an attempt to remove disloyalties and replace them with the president-elect's ideological allies by reclassifying tens of thousands of federal civil service positions as political appointees. This action raises questions regarding the politicization of nonpartisan government posts as well as the establishment of a government machinery that is more devoted to the executive branch than the legal system.

Control of Government Agencies: The idea of imposing party control over important federal agencies, including the Federal Bureau of Investigation (FBI) and the Department of Justice (DOJ), is another controversial element. Project 2025 seeks to restructure the federal bureaucracy in ways that critics claim could jeopardize its efficacy and independence by eliminating organizations like the Department of Homeland Security (DHS) and lowering regulatory monitoring.

Social and Cultural Policies: The project's position on social matters, such as its opposition to diversity initiatives, LGBTQ+ rights, and abortion rights, has drawn criticism for trying to force a particular ideological agenda on the entire nation. These policies are opposed by some who believe they are discriminatory and regressive, going against the ideas of equality and individual rights.

Influence of Religion: Opponents further point out that Project 2025's encouragement of Christian nationalism is problematic since it obfuscates the line between religion and state. The project highlights concern about giving priority to a specific religious perspective in public policy, which may marginalize nonreligious opinions and religious minorities, by endorsing measures that are in line with conservative Christian ideals.

Criticism from Conservative Societies: Remarkably, not every conservative agrees with Project 2025's strategy. Some claim that it deviates from conventional conservative ideas of limited government and free markets and that its proposals—particularly those concerning trade and climate change—could be harmful to global relations and economic growth.

Legal Opposition to Suggested Policies and Their Consequences for the Constitution

In addition to ideological objections, Project 2025 is confronted with substantial legal obstacles that may affect its execution and constitutionality. The project's goals may clash with the executive power constraints and individual rights guaranteed by the U.S. Constitution, which features a system of checks and balances.

Separation of Powers: The idea of separation of powers is at the center of one of the main legal disputes. Critics contend that by centralizing too much power in the executive branch, Project 2025's recommendations—especially those aiming to reduce legislative oversight and increase presidential authority—violate this fundamental tenet.

Executive Orders and Administrative Actions: The project's reliance on these legal tools to implement broad policy changes raises concerns about the extent to which they are appropriate and lawful. Although presidents have broad ability to issue executive orders, any that violate the Constitution or go beyond what is required by statute risk being challenged in court and being declared unlawful.

Constitutional Rights: Some of Project 2025's policies, including limitations on the right to an abortion, protections for LGBTQ+ people, and affirmative action, may be subject to judicial challenges on the grounds of constitutional rights. Courts may carefully examine these practices to determine if they adhere to the equal protection clause of the Fourteenth Amendment, the establishment clause of the First Amendment, and other constitutional provisions that protect individual liberty.

Environmental and Regulatory Rollbacks: Under current environmental laws and international treaties, the project's plans to sever environmental rules and withdraw from international agreements like the Paris Climate Accord may be legally challenged. Courts may assess whether these activities, taking into account their possible effects on public health and the environment, comply with international commitments and legislative requirements.

Civil Liberties and Due Process: Opponents claim that Project 2025's support for policies including enhanced surveillance, the death penalty, and limits on civil liberties may violate the Fifth and Fourteenth Amendment's guarantees of due process. Legal objections may be made to any measures that restrict personal liberties or increase governmental power in ways that jeopardize the right to due process.

Judicial Review and Precedent: Legal challenges to Project 2025 would probably depend on precedents set by earlier court rulings, such as significant instances about federalism, civil rights, and executive authority. The legitimacy and legality of the project's suggested policies would be greatly influenced by the Supreme Court's judgment of these matters.

Under conservative leadership, Project 2025 offers a daring and divisive proposal for reorganizing the federal government. Advocates contend that it is imperative to progress their policy agenda and reinstate principles they believe have been lost, but detractors alert us to the possibility of authoritarian inclinations and constitutional norm violations. The legal obstacles that the project will face, especially about individual rights, the separation of powers, and regulatory authority, will probably influence how it is carried out and whether it complies with constitutional requirements. Project 2025's future depends on judicial review as well as political will, as discussions over these issues highlight deeper conflicts in American politics, democracy, and the rule of law.

CHAPTER 10

FUTURE PROSPECTS AND POLITICAL IMPACT

Project 2025, crafted by the Heritage Foundation, presents a bold vision for reshaping the United States federal government. As the 2024 presidential election looms, the potential scenarios under a Republican administration and the public reception of these proposals become crucial points of analysis.

Scenarios Under a Republican Administration Post-2024

Implementation of Policy Proposals

Should a Republican candidate secure victory in the 2024 election and align with Project 2025's objectives, significant changes across various sectors of governance are anticipated. These changes range from tax cuts and regulatory reforms to profound shifts in social policies and the role of federal agencies.

Economic Reforms: Project 2025 advocates for substantial tax cuts, simplifying the tax code, and potentially adopting protectionist measures. These reforms aim to stimulate economic growth and recalibrate the fiscal landscape towards conservative principles of smaller government and lower taxation. The impact could be profound, affecting everything from individual household finances to corporate investment strategies.

Social and Cultural Policies: The project's stance on issues like abortion, LGBTQ+ rights, and diversity programs indicates a conservative agenda aimed at rolling back progressive gains made in recent decades. This could lead to legislative battles over civil rights, with implications for individual freedoms and social justice.

Environmental and Energy Policies: Under Project 2025, environmental regulations are expected to be relaxed, favoring fossil fuel industries and challenging climate change mitigation efforts. This approach contrasts sharply with global trends toward sustainability and could provoke both domestic and international criticism.

Law Enforcement and National Security: The project's proposals on law enforcement, including the deployment of military for domestic law enforcement, and immigration policies suggest a shift towards stricter controls and potentially controversial measures. These could polarize public opinion and face legal challenges.

Political Dynamics and Legislative Challenges

The implementation of Project 2025 would depend heavily on legislative support and judicial interpretations. Key to its success would be controlling both chambers of Congress to push through sweeping reforms. However, the project's ambitious scope and controversial proposals are likely to face resistance from Democrats, moderate Republicans, and civil society groups.

Legislative Battles: In a divided political landscape, enacting Project 2025's proposals would require navigating complex legislative processes. The project's maximalist approach to executive power and regulatory changes could lead to protracted debates, filibusters, and potential gridlock, affecting its timeline and effectiveness.

Judicial Scrutiny: Many of Project 2025's proposals, particularly those challenging established laws and constitutional interpretations, would almost certainly face legal challenges. The Supreme Court's composition and its interpretation of executive authority and civil liberties would play a pivotal role in shaping the project's implementation.

Public Reception and Political Consequences

Support and Opposition

Conservative Base: Project 2025 is designed to resonate with the conservative base, which views it as a corrective to perceived liberal overreach and government overregulation. Supporters see it as a pathway to restoring traditional values, enhancing national security, and revitalizing the economy through free-market principles.

Critics and Opposition: Conversely, critics argue that Project 2025 represents an authoritarian agenda that undermines democratic norms, civil liberties, and social progress. Opposition would likely mobilize from progressive groups, civil rights advocates, environmentalists, and proponents of governmental checks and balances.

Societal Impact and Cultural Shifts

Impact on Society: The implementation of Project 2025's policies could lead to significant societal shifts. Changes in healthcare access, education policies, and environmental regulations would directly affect millions of Americans, shaping daily life and community dynamics.

Cultural Polarization: The project's stance on cultural issues such as abortion, LGBTQ+ rights, and religious influence in governance could deepen societal divisions. Debates over these issues have historically been contentious, influencing public discourse, electoral outcomes, and the future direction of social norms.

International Perception and Relations

Global Repercussions: Internationally, Project 2025's policies, particularly on trade, climate change, and foreign policy, could strain diplomatic relations. The project's America-first approach and skepticism towards international agreements like the Paris Accord may challenge global cooperation on pressing issues.

Economic Diplomacy: Trade policies advocating protectionism and tariffs could trigger retaliatory measures from trading partners, potentially escalating trade conflicts. This could impact global markets, supply chains, and economic stability, posing challenges for multinational corporations and consumers alike.

A detailed plan for reorganizing the federal government under a hypothetical Republican presidency after 2024 is called Project 2025. Election results, parliamentary wrangling, court interpretations, and public opinion all play a role in its success. Advocates see it as a necessary reform to bring back economic life and conservative principles; detractors warn of authoritarian tendencies and dangers to democratic institutions.

Debates on civil freedoms, constitutional interpretations, presidential power, and social values will all have a significant impact on the political scene after 2024. Project 2025 will continue to have an impact on public discourse and American administration, regardless of whether it becomes a reality or remains a divisive proposition that reflects wider ideological divisions in the country.

A thorough analysis of Project 2025's legislative viability, societal repercussions, and worldwide ramifications is necessary to comprehend its possibilities and political influence. The country finds itself at a turning point as the 2024 election draws near, where divergent ideas on how to prioritize policies and manage the country will determine its future course for years to come.

This study highlights the importance of Project 2025 for American politics and society by offering a thorough examination of the possible outcomes and ramifications of the initiative under a Republican presidency.

CONCLUSION

PROJECT 2025'S POTENTIAL IMPACT ON AMERICAN GOVERNANCE

Project 2025, orchestrated by the Heritage Foundation, represents a comprehensive blueprint aimed at reshaping American governance in alignment with conservative principles. Spanning a wide array of policy domains from taxation and healthcare to law enforcement and environmental regulation, the project outlines a vision that seeks to significantly alter the landscape of federal governance. As we reflect on its potential impact, it becomes evident that Project 2025 not only proposes substantive policy changes but also raises profound questions about the future of democracy and governance in the United States.

Summary of Project 2025's Policy Proposals

The goal of Project 2025's policy agenda is to destroy institutions and laws that are thought to be in the way of conservative rule. Substantial tax cuts and deregulation initiatives, which support business freedoms and minimize federal control, are at the heart of its economic policy. As part of a dedication to supply-side economics and promoting the expansion of the private sector, this also entails the streamlining of tax brackets and the lowering of corporation tax rates.

Project 2025 promotes a more decentralized approach to the healthcare and education sectors by calling for the repeal of the Affordable Care Act and the dissolution of the Department of Education. Social policies propose major legal reforms and rollbacks that are strongly aligned with Christian nationalist beliefs. These policies reflect a conservative perspective on subjects like abortion, LGBTQ+ rights, and diversity programs.

Regarding immigration and law enforcement, the project supports controversial ideas like the use of military forces for domestic law enforcement under the Insurrection Act, strict border security measures, and the reclassification of federal civil servant positions to assure political loyalty.

Environmental policy under Project 2025 is marked by skepticism towards climate change science and a commitment to deregulating industries such as fossil fuels. This includes repealing environmental protections and withdrawing from international agreements aimed at mitigating climate change, reflecting a stark departure from previous administrations' efforts to address environmental challenges.

Broader Implications for Democracy and Governance

Project 2025's implementation would have a significant impact on American democracy and government, affecting fundamental values and standards that support the nation's democratic structure.

Executive Power and Checks on Authority:

The federal government's power structure is called into question by Project 2025's adoption of a maximalist interpretation of the unitary executive theory. The proposal undermines established checks and balances and may jeopardize the constitutionally mandated separation of powers by consolidating authority in the presidency and pushing for the reclassification of civil service jobs.

Rule of Law and Judicial Independence:

Many of Project 2025's recommendations, according to critics, may violate fundamental constitutional rights and be subject to legal challenges. The project's proposals on matters such as immigration, law enforcement, and environmental regulation may put American institutions to the test, especially the judiciary's independence in enforcing the law and interpreting it.

Effect on Social and Cultural Rights:

Project 2025's social policies, which include limitations on the right to an abortion, protections for LGBTQ+ people, and diversity initiatives, pose serious concerns regarding people's liberties and rights. These ideas have the power to alter American culture, possibly marginalizing minority groups and undermining advancements made in the direction of social equality.

Federalism and State Authority:

The project draws attention to conflicts between federal power and state autonomy by advocating for decentralization in industries like healthcare and education. Although Project 2025 advocates for states' rights, its policies may result in differences in the country's regions' access to basic services and legal frameworks.

International Status and Global Diplomacy:

Project 2025's positions on trade and climate change may affect the United States' diplomatic connections and international reputation. Aggressive trade policies and withdrawal from international agreements have the potential to strain relationships and complicate efforts to address global issues, possibly isolating the United States on the international scene.

Considering Democratic Principles and Public Participation

Project 2025 encourages a broader consideration of democratic principles and civic involvement in modern American politics in addition to its specific policy recommendations. The creation and implementation of the initiative demonstrate the impact of interest groups and ideological think tanks on political agendas and election results. It emphasizes how partisan networks and dark money can influence policy formation outside of established political channels.

Furthermore, the way that Project 2025 articulates a conservative vision of government highlights the profound ideological differences that exist within American society. It is a reflection of continuous discussions about the nature of individual rights, the role of the state, and how to strike a balance between security and freedom in a world that is changing quickly. As such, the initiative signals possible routes for future policy discussions and political campaigns and acts as a gauge of ideological shifts within the Republican Party and the larger conservative movement.

To sum up, Project 2025 offers a radical new vision for the American administration that, if implemented, would be a major shift from the standards and practices of the present. Not only would its implementation reshape the federal government's function, but it would also put democratic institutions and constitutional values to the test. It becomes increasingly important to preserve democratic ideals, protect institutional integrity, and encourage educated civic conversation on the future trajectory of American politics as legislators, academics, and citizens grapple with the consequences of Project 2025. The conclusion of these discussions will have a significant impact on how American democracy develops in the future.

Made in the USA
Monee, IL
02 August 2024

63160282R00059